Date:___

3 Good Things

MW00460946

#1

#2

#3

Date:_____
3 Good Things That Happened Today

#1

#2

#3

Date:_____

3 Good Things That Happened Today

#1

#2

#3

Date:_____

3 Good Things That Happened Today

#1

#2

#3

Date:_____

3 Good Things That Happened Today

#1

#2

#3

Date:_____

3 Good Things That Happened Today

#1

#2

#3

Date:_____

3 Good Things That Happened Today

#1

#2

#3

Date:_____

3 Good Things That Happened Today

#1

#2

#3

Date:_____

3 Good Things That Happened Today

#1

#2

#3

Date:_____

3 Good Things That Happened Today

#1

#2

#3

Date:_____

3 Good Things That Happened Today

#1

#2

#3

Date:_____

3 Good Things That Happened Today

#1

#2

#3

Date:_____

3 Good Things That Happened Today

#1

#2

#3

Date:_____
3 Good Things That Happened Today

#1

#2

#3

Date:_____

3 Good Things That Happened Today

#1

#2

#3

Date:_____

3 Good Things That Happened Today

#1

#2

#3

Date:_____

3 Good Things That Happened Today

#1

#2

#3

Date:_____

3 Good Things That Happened Today

#1

#2

#3

Date:_____

3 Good Things That Happened Today

#1

#2

#3

Date:_____

3 Good Things That Happened Today

#1

#2

#3

Date:_____

3 Good Things That Happened Today

#1

#2

#3

Date:_____

3 Good Things That Happened Today

#1

#2

#3

Date:_____

3 Good Things That Happened Today

#1

#2

#3

Date:_____

3 Good Things That Happened Today

#1

#2

#3

Date:_____

3 Good Things That Happened Today

#1

#2

#3

Date:_____

3 Good Things That Happened Today

#1

#2

#3

Date:_____

3 Good Things That Happened Today

#1

#2

#3

Date:_____

3 Good Things That Happened Today

#1

#2

#3

Date:_____

3 Good Things That Happened Today

#1

#2

#3

Date:_____

3 Good Things That Happened Today

#1

#2

#3

Date:_____

3 Good Things That Happened Today

#1

#2

#3

Date:_____

3 Good Things That Happened Today

#1

#2

#3

Date:_____

3 Good Things That Happened Today

#1

#2

#3

Date:_____

3 Good Things That Happened Today

#1

#2

#3

Date:_____

3 Good Things That Happened Today

#1

#2

#3

Date:_____

3 Good Things That Happened Today

#1

#2

#3

Date:_____

3 Good Things That Happened Today

#1

#2

#3

Date:_____

3 Good Things That Happened Today

#1

#2

#3

Date:_____

3 Good Things That Happened Today

#1

#2

#3

Date:_____

3 Good Things That Happened Today

#1

#2

#3

Date:_____

3 Good Things That Happened Today

#1

#2

#3

Date:_____

3 Good Things That Happened Today

#1

#2

#3

Date:_____

3 Good Things That Happened Today

#1

#2

#3

Date:_____

3 Good Things That Happened Today

#1

#2

#3

Date:_____

3 Good Things That Happened Today

#1

#2

#3

Date:_____

3 Good Things That Happened Today

#1

#2

#3

Date:_____

3 Good Things That Happened Today

#1

#2

#3

Date:_____

3 Good Things That Happened Today

#1

#2

#3

Date:_____

3 Good Things That Happened Today

#1

#2

#3

Date:_____

3 Good Things That Happened Today

#1

#2

#3

Date:_____

3 Good Things That Happened Today

#1

#2

#3

Date:_____

3 Good Things That Happened Today

#1

#2

#3

Date:_____

3 Good Things That Happened Today

#1

#2

#3

Date:_____

3 Good Things That Happened Today

#1

#2

#3

Date:_____

3 Good Things That Happened Today

#1

#2

#3

Date:_____

3 Good Things That Happened Today

#1

#2

#3

Date:_____

3 Good Things That Happened Today

#1

#2

#3

Date:_____

3 Good Things That Happened Today

#1

#2

#3

Date:_____

3 Good Things That Happened Today

#1

#2

#3

Date:_____

3 Good Things That Happened Today

#1

#2

#3

Date:_____

3 Good Things That Happened Today

#1

#2

#3

Date:_____

3 Good Things That Happened Today

#1

#2

#3

Date:_____

3 Good Things That Happened Today

#1

#2

#3

Date:_____

3 Good Things That Happened Today

#1

#2

#3

Date:_____

3 Good Things That Happened Today

#1

#2

#3

Date:_____

3 Good Things That Happened Today

#1

#2

#3

Date:_____

3 Good Things That Happened Today

#1

#2

#3

Date:_____

3 Good Things That Happened Today

#1

#2

#3

Date:_____

3 Good Things That Happened Today

#1

#2

#3

Date:_____

3 Good Things That Happened Today

#1

#2

#3

Date:_____

3 Good Things That Happened Today

#1

#2

#3

Date:_____

3 Good Things That Happened Today

#1

#2

#3

Date:_____

3 Good Things That Happened Today

#1

#2

#3

Date:_____

3 Good Things That Happened Today

#1

#2

#3

Date:_____

3 Good Things That Happened Today

#1

#2

#3

Date:_____

3 Good Things That Happened Today

#1

#2

#3

Date:_____

3 Good Things That Happened Today

#1

#2

#3

Date:_____

3 Good Things That Happened Today

#1

#2

#3

Date:_____

3 Good Things That Happened Today

#1

#2

#3

Date:_____

3 Good Things That Happened Today

#1

#2

#3

Date:_____

3 Good Things That Happened Today

#1

#2

#3

Date:_____

3 Good Things That Happened Today

#1

#2

#3

Date:_____

3 Good Things That Happened Today

#1

#2

#3

Date:_____

3 Good Things That Happened Today

#1

#2

#3

Date:_____
3 Good Things That Happened Today

#1

#2

#3

Date:_____

3 Good Things That Happened Today

#1

#2

#3

Date:_____

3 Good Things That Happened Today

#1

#2

#3

Date:_____

3 Good Things That Happened Today

#1

#2

#3

Date:_____

3 Good Things That Happened Today

#1

#2

#3

Date:_____

3 Good Things That Happened Today

#1

#2

#3

Date:_____

3 Good Things That Happened Today

#1

#2

#3

Date:_____

3 Good Things That Happened Today

#1

#2

#3

Date:_____

3 Good Things That Happened Today

#1

#2

#3

Date:_____

3 Good Things That Happened Today

#1

#2

#3

Date:_____

3 Good Things That Happened Today

#1

#2

#3

Date:_____

3 Good Things That Happened Today

#1

#2

#3

Date:_____

3 Good Things That Happened Today

#1

#2

#3

Date:_____

3 Good Things That Happened Today

#1

#2

#3

Date:_____

3 Good Things That Happened Today

#1

#2

#3

Date:_____

3 Good Things That Happened Today

#1

#2

#3

Date:_____

3 Good Things That Happened Today

#1

#2

#3

Date:_____

3 Good Things That Happened Today

#1

#2

#3

Date:_____

3 Good Things That Happened Today

#1

#2

#3

Date:_____

3 Good Things That Happened Today

#1

#2

#3

Date:_____

3 Good Things That Happened Today

#1

#2

#3

Date:_____

3 Good Things That Happened Today

#1

#2

#3

Date:_____

3 Good Things That Happened Today

#1

#2

#3

Date:_____

3 Good Things That Happened Today

#1

#2

#3

Date:_____

3 Good Things That Happened Today

#1

#2

#3

Date:_____

3 Good Things That Happened Today

#1
#2
#3

Date:_____

3 Good Things That Happened Today

#1

#2

#3

Date:_____

3 Good Things That Happened Today

#1

#2

#3

Date:_____

3 Good Things That Happened Today

#1

#2

#3

Date:_____

3 Good Things That Happened Today

#1

#2

#3

Date:_____

3 Good Things That Happened Today

#1

#2

#3

Date:_____

3 Good Things That Happened Today

#1

#2

#3

Date:_____

3 Good Things That Happened Today

#1

#2

#3

Date:_____

3 Good Things That Happened Today

#1

#2

#3

Date:_____

3 Good Things That Happened Today

#1

#2

#3

Date:_____

3 Good Things That Happened Today

#1

#2

#3

Date:_____

3 Good Things That Happened Today

#1

#2

#3

Date:_____

3 Good Things That Happened Today

#1

#2

#3

Date:_____

3 Good Things That Happened Today

#1

#2

#3

Date:_____

3 Good Things That Happened Today

#1

#2

#3

Date:_____

3 Good Things That Happened Today

#1

#2

#3

Date:_____

3 Good Things That Happened Today

#1

#2

#3

Date:_____

3 Good Things That Happened Today

#1

#2

#3

Date:_____

3 Good Things That Happened Today

#1

#2

#3

Date:_____

3 Good Things That Happened Today

#1

#2

#3

Date:_____

3 Good Things That Happened Today

#1

#2

#3

Date:_____

3 Good Things That Happened Today

#1

#2

#3

Date:_____

3 Good Things That Happened Today

#1

#2

#3

Date:_____

3 Good Things That Happened Today

#1

#2

#3

Date:_____

3 Good Things That Happened Today

#1

#2

#3

Date:_____

3 Good Things That Happened Today

#1

#2

#3

Date:_____

3 Good Things That Happened Today

#1

#2

#3

Date:_____

3 Good Things That Happened Today

#1

#2

#3

Date:_____

3 Good Things That Happened Today

#1

#2

#3

Date:_____

3 Good Things That Happened Today

#1

#2

#3

Date:_____

3 Good Things That Happened Today

#1

#2

#3

Date:_____

3 Good Things That Happened Today

#1

#2

#3

Date:_____

3 Good Things That Happened Today

#1

#2

#3

Date:_____

3 Good Things That Happened Today

#1

#2

#3

Date:_____

3 Good Things That Happened Today

#1

#2

#3

Date:_____

3 Good Things That Happened Today

#1

#2

#3

Date:_____

3 Good Things That Happened Today

#1

#2

#3

Date:_____

3 Good Things That Happened Today

#1

#2

#3

Date:_____

3 Good Things That Happened Today

#1

#2

#3

Date:_____

3 Good Things That Happened Today

#1

#2

#3

Date:_____

3 Good Things That Happened Today

#1

#2

#3

Date:_____

3 Good Things That Happened Today

#1

#2

#3

Date:_____

3 Good Things That Happened Today

#1

#2

#3

Date:_____

3 Good Things That Happened Today

#1

#2

#3

Date:_____

3 Good Things That Happened Today

#1

#2

#3

Date:_____

3 Good Things That Happened Today

#1

#2

#3

Date:_____

3 Good Things That Happened Today

#1

#2

#3

Date:_____

3 Good Things That Happened Today

#1

#2

#3

Date:_____

3 Good Things That Happened Today

#1

#2

#3

Date:_____

3 Good Things That Happened Today

#1

#2

#3

Date:_____

3 Good Things That Happened Today

#1

#2

#3

Date:_____

3 Good Things That Happened Today

#1

#2

#3

Date:_____

3 Good Things That Happened Today

#1

#2

#3

Date:_____

3 Good Things That Happened Today

#1

#2

#3

Date:_____

3 Good Things That Happened Today

#1

#2

#3

Date:_____

3 Good Things That Happened Today

#1

#2

#3

Date:_____

3 Good Things That Happened Today

#1

#2

#3

Date:_____

3 Good Things That Happened Today

#1

#2

#3

Date:_____

3 Good Things That Happened Today

#1

#2

#3

Date:_____

3 Good Things That Happened Today

#1

#2

#3

Date:_____

3 Good Things That Happened Today

#1

#2

#3

Date:_____

3 Good Things That Happened Today

#1

#2

#3

Date:_____

3 Good Things That Happened Today

#1

#2

#3

Date:_____

3 Good Things That Happened Today

#1

#2

#3

Date:_____

3 Good Things That Happened Today

#1

#2

#3

Date:_____

3 Good Things That Happened Today

#1

#2

#3

Date:_____

3 Good Things That Happened Today

#1

#2

#3

Date:_____

3 Good Things That Happened Today

#1

#2

#3

Date:_____

3 Good Things That Happened Today

#1

#2

#3

Date:_____

3 Good Things That Happened Today

#1

#2

#3

Date:_____

3 Good Things That Happened Today

#1

#2

#3

Date:_____

3 Good Things That Happened Today

#1

#2

#3

Date:_____

3 Good Things That Happened Today

#1

#2

#3

Date:_____

3 Good Things That Happened Today

#1

#2

#3

Date:_____

3 Good Things That Happened Today

#1

#2

#3

Date:_____

3 Good Things That Happened Today

#1

#2

#3

Date:_____

3 Good Things That Happened Today

#1

#2

#3

Date:_____

3 Good Things That Happened Today

#1

#2

#3

Date:_____

3 Good Things That Happened Today

#1

#2

#3

Date:_____

3 Good Things That Happened Today

#1

#2

#3

Date:_____

3 Good Things That Happened Today

#1

#2

#3

Date:_____

3 Good Things That Happened Today

#1

#2

#3

Date:_____

3 Good Things That Happened Today

#1

#2

#3

Date:_____

3 Good Things That Happened Today

#1

#2

#3

Date:_____

3 Good Things That Happened Today

#1

#2

#3

Date:_____

3 Good Things That Happened Today

#1

#2

#3

Date:_____

3 Good Things That Happened Today

#1

#2

#3

Date:_____

3 Good Things That Happened Today

#1

#2

#3

Date:_____

3 Good Things That Happened Today

#1

#2

#3

Date:_____

3 Good Things That Happened Today

#1

#2

#3

Date:_____

3 Good Things That Happened Today

#1

#2

#3

Made in the USA
Columbia, SC
07 December 2020

26745103R00111